IGNOTUS

# AI Toolkit for Entrepreneurs

*Build, Scale, and Succeed*

First edition

ISBN: 979-8-9922631-5-2

This book was professionally typeset on Reedsy.
Find out more at reedsy.com

# Contents

VII  Bonus Section: Apps to Elevate Your Creativity
and Content

# Introduction

The future of entrepreneurship is here, and it's powered by artificial intelligence. Once the stuff of science fiction, AI has quickly become an essential tool for modern business. Whether you're a solopreneur launching your first venture or a seasoned business owner looking to stay ahead, AI tools can give you the edge you need to grow, scale, and succeed faster than ever before.

This book, *AI Toolkit for Nex-Gen Entrepreneurs: To Build, Scale, and Succeed*, is your guide to navigating the exciting world of AI. Think of it as your personal roadmap to the best AI tools available today. These tools are designed to simplify your workflow, supercharge your creativity, and help you achieve more in less time. And the best part? You don't need to be a tech wizard to use them.

Why AI Matters for Entrepreneurs

Running a business is demanding. From marketing and sales to operations and customer support, there are countless moving parts to manage. This is where AI comes in. By automating repetitive tasks, generating insights from data, and even assisting with creative projects, AI tools free up your time so you can focus on what really matters: growing your business.

Here are just a few ways AI can transform your entrepreneurial journey:

- **Boost Efficiency:** Automate tasks like email responses, social media posts, and customer inquiries.

- **Enhance Creativity:** Use AI to design stunning visuals, write compelling copy, and generate innovative ideas.
- **Drive Sales:** Leverage AI-powered marketing tools to reach the right audience and close deals faster.
- **Stay Competitive:** Keep up with industry trends and make data-driven decisions with AI insights.

How This Book Will Help You

This book is not just a list of tools—it's a practical guide to using them effectively. Each chapter introduces a specific AI tool, explains what it does, and provides actionable tips to get started. You'll also find real-life examples to inspire you and help you see how these tools can be applied to your own business.

Whether you're looking to create engaging social media content, streamline your e-commerce operations, or improve customer engagement, this book has you covered. The tools featured here are accessible, affordable, and ready to integrate into your business today.

What to Expect

- **Quick and Easy:** This book is designed for busy entrepreneurs. Each chapter is concise and actionable, so you can learn on the go and start applying what you've learned immediately.
- **The Best Tools:** From AI writing assistants like ChatGPT to marketing platforms like AdCreative.ai, we've selected the top tools across multiple categories to cover all your business needs.
- **No Technical Jargon:** You don't need a tech background to benefit from this book. Every tool is explained in simple terms, with clear instructions on how to use it.

Who This Book Is For

- **Aspiring Entrepreneurs:** If you're just starting out, these tools will give you a head start by automating tedious tasks and helping you focus on strategy.
- **Small Business Owners:** Streamline operations, improve customer experiences, and grow your sales with AI.
- **Freelancers and Solopreneurs:** Maximize your productivity and creativity without the need for a big team.
- **Seasoned Entrepreneurs:** Stay competitive and explore new opportunities by integrating AI into your workflow.

The tools covered in this book are transforming industries, and now they're ready to transform your business. Let's dive in and discover how AI can help you grow, scale, and succeed!

# AI, Applications and Marketing Tools

## Core AI Tools

- ChatGPT: Your AI Writing and Brainstorming Assistant
- Canva: Simplifying Design for Entrepreneurs
- DALL·E: Turning Text into Stunning Visuals
- Grammarly: Writing Clearly and Professionally
- Zapier: Automating Workflows to Save Time

## Creative and Visual Tools

- Adobe Firefly: Revolutionizing Design with AI
- Runway ML: AI-Powered Video Editing
- MidJourney: Creating Artistic Visuals
- Synthesia: AI Avatars for Video Creation
- Pictory.ai: Repurposing Content into Videos
- AdCreative.ai: High-Performing Ad Design
- Descript: Podcast and Video Editing Made Easy

## Productivity and Business Tools

- Notion AI: Managing Tasks and Ideas with AI
- GitHub Copilot: AI for Smarter Coding
- Tidio AI: Enhancing Customer Support with Chatbots
- Otter.ai: Automatic Meeting Transcriptions

- Wirestock: Simplifying Content Monetization
- Reedsy: Your Partner in Book Writing and Publishing
- Reface: AI-Powered Personal Avatars and Fun Visuals
- iPlan.ai: AI-Powered Travel Planning Made Simple

**Conclusion**

- Recap of Tools and Their Applications
- How to Integrate AI into Your Daily Workflow
- Future Trends in AI for Entrepreneurs

The tools covered in this book are transforming industries, and now they're ready to transform your business. Let's dive in and discover how AI can help you grow, scale, and succeed!

# I

# Core AI Tools

*AI tools are essential for entrepreneurs, streamlining workflows, enhancing creativity, and saving time. They simplify tasks, automate processes, and provide insights, enabling users to focus on growth. From improving communication to generating content and automating operations, these tools offer innovative solutions to everyday challenges. Versatile and user-friendly, they form a solid foundation for building and scaling businesses efficiently in a competitive landscape.*

# 1

# ChatGPT – Your AI Writing and Brainstorming Assistant

What is ChatGPT?

ChatGPT, developed by OpenAI, is a powerful AI language model that can engage in human-like conversations, generate text, and assist with countless tasks. Think of it as your personal assistant for writing, brainstorming, and problem-solving. Whether you need to draft an email, generate creative ideas, or summarize a document, ChatGPT is always ready to help.

Why Use ChatGPT?

As an entrepreneur, time and efficiency are crucial. ChatGPT saves you from spending hours on tasks that can be automated or simplified. Here are some of the key benefits:

- **Content Creation:** Generate high-quality blog posts, social media captions, and marketing emails in seconds.
- **Brainstorming:** Need fresh ideas? ChatGPT can help you explore new concepts or refine existing ones.
- **Learning and Research:** Get concise explanations, summaries, or insights into complex topics.

- **Problem-Solving:** Whether you're drafting a proposal or troubleshooting a business issue, ChatGPT can guide you.

Who Should Use ChatGPT?

ChatGPT is ideal for:

- **Freelancers and Solopreneurs:** Quickly create professional content without hiring a writer.
- **Small Business Owners:** Save time on repetitive writing tasks.
- **Creatives:** Get inspiration and ideas for projects.
- **Students and Researchers:** Simplify learning and research tasks.

Getting Started with ChatGPT

Here's how you can start using ChatGPT today:

1. **Sign Up:** Visit chat.openai.com and create an account.
2. **Ask a Question:** Simply type your query or request, such as "Draft an email to a potential client introducing my services."
3. **Refine the Response:** Review and edit the output to suit your tone and preferences.
4. **Explore Use Cases:** Experiment with different prompts, from brainstorming business names to drafting detailed reports.

Pro Tips

- **Be Specific:** The more detailed your prompt, the better the response. For example, instead of "Write a blog post," try "Write a 500-word blog post about the benefits of using AI tools in small businesses."
- **Iterate:** If the response isn't quite right, provide feedback or ask for a revision. ChatGPT improves with context.
- **Experiment:** Use ChatGPT for tasks beyond writing, such as learning

new skills or generating creative solutions.

Real-Life Example

**Scenario:** A small business owner needs a marketing email to promote a new product.

**Prompt:** "Write a marketing email for a 20% discount on eco-friendly water bottles. Include a catchy subject line, a brief description of the product's benefits, and a call to action."

**Output:***Subject Line:* "Stay Hydrated, Stay Green – 20% Off Today Only!"

*Body:* Discover the perfect way to stay hydrated while helping the planet. Our eco-friendly water bottles are made from sustainable materials, designed to keep your drinks cold for 24 hours. Don't miss out on this exclusive offer – 20% off for a limited time! Click below to grab yours now.

*Call to Action:* [Shop Now]

Final Thoughts

ChatGPT is a versatile tool that can handle a wide range of tasks, making it an invaluable asset for entrepreneurs. Whether you're streamlining your operations, creating content, or brainstorming your next big idea, ChatGPT is here to help. The more you use it, the more ways you'll discover to integrate it into your business workflow.

# 2

# Canva – Simplifying Design for Entrepreneurs

What is Canva?

Canva is an online graphic design platform that makes creating professional-quality visuals simple, even if you have no design experience. With its drag-and-drop interface and a vast library of templates, Canva is the go-to tool for entrepreneurs looking to create stunning graphics quickly and affordably.

Why Use Canva?

Visual content is crucial for branding and marketing, but not everyone has the time or budget to hire a professional designer. Canva bridges the gap by providing easy-to-use tools that let you design like a pro. Key benefits include:

- **Templates for Everything:** From social media posts to business cards, Canva offers templates for nearly every design need.
- **User-Friendly Interface:** Its drag-and-drop design makes it accessible to anyone.
- **Affordable and Scalable:** Canva offers a free version with plenty of features, while the Pro plan unlocks premium assets and tools.
- **Brand Consistency:** Save your brand colors, fonts, and logos for

consistent designs across all platforms.

## Who Should Use Canva?

Canva is ideal for:

- **Entrepreneurs and Small Business Owners:** Create marketing materials, pitch decks, and more.
- **Social Media Managers:** Design eye-catching posts, stories, and ads.
- **Freelancers and Solopreneurs:** Maintain a professional image with polished visuals.
- **Educators and Nonprofits:** Produce engaging presentations and materials.

## Getting Started with Canva

Here's how to start designing with Canva:

1. **Sign Up:** Visit canva.com and create a free account.
2. **Choose a Template:** Select a template that suits your needs (e.g., Instagram post, flyer, or presentation).
3. **Customize:** Use the drag-and-drop editor to add text, images, and other elements. You can upload your own assets or use Canva's library of free and premium resources.
4. **Download and Share:** Once your design is ready, download it in your preferred format or share it directly to social media.

## Pro Tips

- **Use Canva's AI Tools:** Features like Magic Resize let you quickly adapt a design for multiple platforms.
- **Collaborate with Your Team:** Share designs and work on projects

together in real time.

- **Leverage Free Resources:** Canva's free plan includes thousands of templates, photos, and icons to get you started.

Real-Life Example

**Scenario:** A solopreneur wants to create a professional Instagram post to promote a new product launch.

**Steps:**

1. Choose an Instagram post template from Canva's library.
2. Add a product photo and customize the text with a catchy headline like, "New Product Alert!"
3. Use Canva's free icons and elements to enhance the design.
4. Export the finished post and upload it to Instagram.

**Result:** A polished, eye-catching post ready to grab attention and drive sales.

Final Thoughts

Canva is a must-have tool for entrepreneurs who want to create professional visuals without spending a fortune. Whether you're designing a logo, a social media post, or a presentation, Canva's intuitive interface and vast resources make it easier than ever to bring your ideas to life.

# 3

# DALL·E – Turning Text into Stunning Visuals

What is DALL·E?

DALL·E, developed by OpenAI, is an AI tool that transforms text prompts into high-quality images. It's perfect for entrepreneurs who need unique visuals for marketing, branding, or creative projects but don't have the time or resources for custom design work.

Why Use DALL·E?

Creating compelling visuals can be time-consuming and expensive. DALL·E simplifies the process by generating stunning images based on simple text descriptions. Here's how it can help:

- **Save Time:** Generate unique images in seconds without the need for design skills.
- **Affordable Creativity:** Avoid the costs of hiring a designer or purchasing stock photos.
- **Unlimited Possibilities:** From realistic photos to imaginative artwork, DALL·E can create almost anything you describe.

Who Should Use DALL·E?

DALL·E is ideal for:

- **Marketers and Advertisers:** Quickly create eye-catching visuals for campaigns.
- **Small Business Owners:** Generate product images, social media content, or website banners.
- **Creatives:** Explore artistic concepts and bring ideas to life.
- **Educators and Content Creators:** Produce visuals to enhance presentations, videos, and learning materials.

Getting Started with DALL·E

Here's how to begin using DALL·E:

1. **Access the Tool:** Visit openai.com/dall-e and sign in.
2. **Write a Prompt:** Describe the image you want. For example, "A futuristic cityscape at sunset with flying cars."
3. **Generate Images:** DALL·E will produce several options based on your description.
4. **Download and Use:** Choose the image you like and download it for your project.

Pro Tips

- **Be Specific:** The more detailed your description, the better the results. Include elements like style, color, and composition.
- **Experiment:** Try different prompts to explore creative possibilities and refine your vision.
- **Combine with Other Tools:** Use Canva to edit and integrate DALL·E-generated images into your designs.

Real-Life Example

**Scenario:** A startup founder needs a unique header image for their website.

**Prompt:** "A minimalist illustration of a rocket launching into space, with a glowing earth in the background."

**Result:** DALL·E generates multiple high-quality illustrations, and the founder selects one that perfectly aligns with their brand. The image is uploaded to the website header, creating a professional and engaging look.

Final Thoughts

DALL·E is a revolutionary tool for entrepreneurs who want to elevate their visual content. By turning your ideas into reality with just a text prompt, it removes the barriers to high-quality design and opens up endless creative possibilities.

# 4

# Grammarly – Writing Clearly and Professionally

What is Grammarly?

Grammarly is an AI-powered writing assistant that helps you write clearly, confidently, and error-free. From emails to social media posts, Grammarly ensures your message is professional and polished, making it a must-have tool for entrepreneurs and professionals alike.

Why Use Grammarly?

Effective communication is key to business success. Grammarly saves time by catching errors, improving tone, and suggesting better word choices. Benefits include:

- **Error-Free Writing:** Detect and correct grammar, spelling, and punctuation mistakes.
- **Tone Adjustment:** Ensure your writing matches your audience— formal, casual, or persuasive.
- **Clarity Suggestions:** Simplify complex sentences to improve readability.

Who Should Use Grammarly?

Grammarly is ideal for:

- **Entrepreneurs and Business Owners:** Write professional emails, proposals, and reports.
- **Freelancers:** Ensure clear and error-free client communications.
- **Content Creators:** Polish blog posts, articles, and social media captions.
- **Students and Academics:** Refine essays, papers, and presentations.

Getting Started with Grammarly

Here's how to get started:

1. **Install the Tool:** Visit grammarly.com to sign up. Install the browser extension or desktop app for seamless integration.
2. **Start Writing:** Grammarly works automatically, highlighting errors and suggesting improvements as you type.
3. **Refine with AI:** Use advanced suggestions to improve tone, clarity, and word choice.
4. **Explore Premium Features:** Upgrade to unlock tools like plagiarism detection and style guides.

Pro Tips

- **Use the Tone Detector:** Ensure your message resonates with the intended audience.
- **Integrate Everywhere:** Grammarly works with email platforms, word processors, and even social media sites.
- **Review Suggestions:** Double-check Grammarly's recommendations to ensure they align with your intent.

Real-Life Example

**Scenario:** An entrepreneur is writing a funding proposal for investors.
**Steps:**

1. Draft the proposal in a word processor.
2. Use Grammarly to identify and fix grammar and clarity issues.
3. Refine the tone to ensure it's formal and persuasive.
4. Submit the polished proposal with confidence.

**Result:** The entrepreneur impresses investors with a professional and well-written proposal.

Final Thoughts

Grammarly is an essential tool for anyone who wants to communicate effectively and professionally. With its powerful AI, you can write with confidence, knowing your message is clear and impactful.

# 5

# Zapier – Automating Workflows to Save Time

What is Zapier?

Zapier is an automation tool that connects your favorite apps and services, enabling them to work together seamlessly. With Zapier, you can automate repetitive tasks and focus on what matters most—growing your business.

Why Use Zapier?

As an entrepreneur, efficiency is everything. Zapier eliminates manual work by automating workflows between apps, saving you time and reducing errors. Key benefits include:

- **Task Automation:** Automate data entry, email notifications, and file management.
- **App Integration:** Connect over 2,000 apps, including Gmail, Slack, and Trello.
- **Custom Workflows:** Create Zaps (automations) tailored to your specific needs.

Who Should Use Zapier?

Zapier is ideal for:

- **Small Business Owners:** Automate administrative tasks like invoicing and lead tracking.
- **Marketers:** Sync social media posts, email campaigns, and analytics.
- **Freelancers:** Streamline project management and client communications.
- **Teams:** Improve collaboration by connecting apps used across departments.

Getting Started with Zapier

Here's how to start automating with Zapier:

1. **Sign Up:** Visit zapier.com and create a free account.
2. **Choose a Trigger:** Select an app and action to start your workflow (e.g., "When I receive an email in Gmail...").
3. **Define an Action:** Specify what happens next (e.g., "...save the email to Trello as a task").
4. **Test and Activate:** Run the Zap to ensure it works, then turn it on to start automating.

Pro Tips

- **Start Simple:** Begin with basic Zaps and gradually create more complex workflows.
- **Explore Templates:** Use Zapier's pre-made workflows for common tasks.
- **Monitor Activity:** Check your Zap history to troubleshoot issues and optimize performance.

Real-Life Example

**Scenario:** A marketer wants to track new leads from a website form.
**Steps:**

1. Set the form submission as the trigger.
2. Connect it to Google Sheets to log each lead.
3. Add an action to notify the sales team via Slack.
4. Test the workflow and activate the Zap.

**Result:** The marketer saves hours each week by automating lead tracking and communication.

Final Thoughts

Zapier empowers entrepreneurs to work smarter, not harder. By automating repetitive tasks and connecting your favorite apps, you can save time, reduce errors, and focus on growing your business.

# II

# Creative and Visual Tools

*AI-powered creative tools revolutionize content creation, enabling stunning visuals, professional video editing, and engaging ads. They simplify repurposing content, crafting lifelike avatars, and enhancing storytelling with ease. These tools empower entrepreneurs and creators to streamline workflows, produce high-quality visuals, and explore innovative possibilities, transforming how ideas come to life in the digital age.*

# 6

# Adobe Firefly – Revolutionizing Design with AI

What is Adobe Firefly?

Adobe Firefly is a suite of generative AI tools integrated into Adobe Creative Cloud, designed to simplify and enhance the creative process for designers, marketers, and content creators.

Why Use Adobe Firefly?

Firefly makes advanced design features accessible, even to non-designers. Key benefits include:

- **Generative Image Creation:** Transform text prompts into professional-quality images.
- **AI-Enhanced Editing:** Automate tasks like background removal and content-aware fills.
- **Text Effects:** Create stylized text visuals for branding and marketing materials.

Who Should Use Adobe Firefly?

- **Design Professionals:** Speed up workflows with AI-assisted editing tools.

- **Small Business Owners:** Produce high-quality visuals for websites, ads, and presentations.
- **Marketers:** Generate social media assets and promotional materials.

Getting Started with Adobe Firefly

1. **Access the Tool:** Log in to your Adobe Creative Cloud account.
2. **Explore Features:** Test Firefly's AI tools, including text-to-image generation.
3. **Enhance Your Workflows:** Use AI features to refine designs quickly.

Pro Tips

- Experiment with different text prompts to unlock creative possibilities.
- Combine Firefly with other Adobe tools for seamless project integration.

Real-Life Example

**Scenario:** A business owner creates promotional graphics for a product launch using Firefly.

Final Thoughts

Firefly empowers users to create professional designs with ease, saving time and boosting creativity.

# 7

# Runway ML – AI-Powered Video Editing

What is Runway ML?

Runway ML is a cutting-edge AI tool that simplifies video editing and creative content production. It offers advanced features like background removal, text-to-video generation, and real-time collaboration, making it an ideal choice for creators and entrepreneurs.

Why Use Runway ML?

Creating professional-quality videos can be time-intensive, but Runway ML accelerates the process with AI. Benefits include:

- **Real-Time Background Removal:** Eliminate backgrounds without a green screen.
- **Text-to-Video Generation:** Quickly turn written concepts into video content.
- **Collaboration Tools:** Work with teams in real-time.

Who Should Use Runway ML?

- **Video Creators:** Simplify editing processes and focus on creativity.
- **Marketers:** Produce promotional videos with minimal effort.

- **Small Business Owners:** Create engaging video content for social media and ads.

Getting Started with Runway ML

1. **Sign Up:** Visit runwayml.com to create an account.
2. **Upload Your Footage:** Import your video clips.
3. **Use AI Features:** Experiment with tools like background removal and automatic editing.
4. **Export and Share:** Download your final video or share it directly to social media.

Pro Tips

- Combine Runway ML with traditional editing software for enhanced capabilities.
- Use text-to-video for quick concept presentations or explainer videos.

Real-Life Example

**Scenario:** A business owner needs a quick promotional video for a new product.

**Steps:**

1. Upload product images and short clips to Runway ML.
2. Use text-to-video to add animated descriptions.
3. Remove backgrounds for a clean and professional look.
4. Export and share the final video on social media platforms.

**Result:** A polished and engaging video ready to capture audience attention.

## Final Thoughts

Runway ML simplifies video editing with AI, enabling creators and businesses to produce high-quality content efficiently while unlocking new creative possibilities

# 8

# MidJourney – Creating Artistic Visuals

What is MidJourney?

MidJourney is an AI-powered platform that generates artistic and imaginative visuals from text prompts. Whether you need concept art, unique designs, or abstract imagery, MidJourney brings your ideas to life.

Why Use MidJourney?

MidJourney offers unparalleled creative freedom. Benefits include:

- **Unique Art Styles:** Explore various artistic styles for your projects.
- **Fast Prototyping:** Quickly visualize concepts without hiring a designer.
- **Customizable Outputs:** Refine generated visuals to match your vision.

Who Should Use MidJourney?

- **Artists and Designers:** Explore new styles and techniques.
- **Marketers:** Generate eye-catching visuals for campaigns.
- **Entrepreneurs:** Create logos, banners, or abstract art for branding.

Getting Started with MidJourney

1. **Access the Tool:** Visit midjourney.com and join their Discord server.
2. **Enter a Prompt:** Describe your desired image in detail (e.g., "a futuristic cityscape with neon lights").
3. **Refine Your Output:** Use variations to adjust the generated visuals.
4. **Download and Use:** Save the final image for your project.

Pro Tips

· Experiment with different prompts to discover unexpected results.
· Combine MidJourney visuals with editing tools like Canva for enhanced designs.

Real-Life Example

**Scenario:** An entrepreneur needs abstract visuals for a new product line.

**Steps:**

1. Enter prompts like "abstract geometric patterns in pastel colors."
2. Select and refine a generated image.
3. Use the image in product packaging and marketing materials.

**Result:** A distinctive and professional design that elevates the brand's appeal.

Final Thoughts

MidJourney transforms text prompts into stunning visuals, offering endless creative possibilities for designers, marketers, and creatives.

# 9

# Synthesia – AI Avatars for Video Creation

What is Synthesia?

Synthesia lets you create professional videos featuring lifelike AI avatars. It's an ideal solution for training materials, marketing videos, and personalized communication.

Why Use Synthesia?

- **Customizable Avatars:** Choose or create avatars that fit your brand.
- **Script-Based Videos:** Generate videos quickly by uploading text.
- **Multi-Language Support:** Produce content in multiple languages with accurate pronunciations.

Who Should Use Synthesia?

- **Educators:** Develop engaging online courses.
- **Marketers:** Add a human touch to ad campaigns.
- **Businesses:** Create internal training videos efficiently.

Getting Started with Synthesia

1. Visit synthesia.io and create an account.
2. Select an avatar or customize one.
3. Upload your script and choose a language.
4. Download and distribute your video.

Pro Tips

· Use avatars for personalized onboarding videos.
· Leverage multilingual capabilities for global audiences.

Real-Life Example

A company creates a welcome video for new hires in multiple languages, using Synthesia's customizable avatars to save time and resources.

Final Thoughts

Synthesia simplifies video creation with lifelike AI avatars, making it an efficient tool for training, marketing, and personalized communication.

# 10

# Pictory.ai – Transforming Content into Videos

What is Pictory.ai?

Pictory.ai converts written content into engaging video summaries. Whether you're repurposing a blog post or creating social media content, Pictory makes the process simple and effective.

Why Use Pictory.ai?

Pictory saves time and maximizes content reach with features like:

- **Automated Video Creation:** Turn articles or transcripts into short videos.
- **Customizable Templates:** Use pre-designed templates for a polished look.
- **Text-to-Video:** Highlight key points from written content in an engaging format.

Who Should Use Pictory.ai?

- **Content Marketers:** Repurpose blog posts into video content.
- **Social Media Managers:** Create bite-sized videos for platforms like Instagram or TikTok.

- **Entrepreneurs:** Share video summaries of long-form content.

Getting Started with Pictory.ai

1. **Sign Up:** Visit pictory.ai to create an account.
2. **Upload Your Content:** Import a blog post, transcript, or text document.
3. **Customize the Video:** Select a template and adjust visuals, text, and music.
4. **Export and Share:** Download the video or share it directly to social platforms.

Pro Tips

- Use Pictory to create teaser videos for blog posts or eBooks.
- Add captions to improve accessibility and engagement.

Real-Life Example

**Scenario:** A content marketer wants to promote a blog post on social media.

**Steps:**

1. Import the blog URL into Pictory.
2. Highlight key points to include in the video.
3. Customize visuals and add background music.
4. Share the video on Instagram and LinkedIn.

**Result:** Increased engagement and traffic to the original blog post.

Final Thoughts

Pictory AI transforms text into engaging videos, making it a fast and effective tool for content repurposing and social media marketing.

# 11

# AdCreative.ai – High-Performing Ad Design

What is AdCreative.ai?

AdCreative.ai is a powerful tool that generates engaging ad creatives and copy tailored to your target audience. It uses AI to analyze your goals and produce optimized ads that drive conversions.

Why Use AdCreative.ai?

Creating effective ads can be time-consuming and expensive. AdCreative.ai simplifies the process with:

- **Optimized Designs:** AI-driven suggestions for ad layouts and visuals.
- **Conversion-Ready Copy:** Generate headlines and descriptions tailored to your campaign.
- **Multi-Platform Compatibility:** Design ads for Facebook, Google, Instagram, and more.

Who Should Use AdCreative.ai?

- **Marketers:** Save time on ad creation and improve ROI.
- **Small Businesses:** Access professional-quality ads without hiring

an agency.

- **Entrepreneurs:** Quickly test multiple ad variations to find what works best.

Getting Started with AdCreative.ai

1. **Sign Up:** Visit adcreative.ai to create an account.
2. **Set Goals:** Define your campaign objectives.
3. **Generate Ads:** Enter details like target audience and key messages.
4. **Download and Launch:** Export your ads and upload them to your chosen platform.

Pro Tips

- Use A/B testing to compare different ad variations.
- Customize AI-generated suggestions to align with your brand voice.

Real-Life Example

**Scenario:** A startup needs Facebook ads for a product launch.

**Steps:**

1. Enter details about the product and audience.
2. Generate multiple ad creatives with headlines and images.
3. Select the best-performing ad and launch the campaign.

**Result:** Increased click-through rates and engagement with minimal effort.

Final Thoughts

AdCreative.ai streamlines ad creation with AI, delivering optimized visuals and copy for improved engagement and conversions.

# 12

# Descript – Simplifying Video and Audio Editing

What is Descript?

Descript is an all-in-one platform for editing video and audio content. It combines text-based editing, transcription, and screen recording features to streamline the content creation process.

Why Use Descript?

Descript makes editing accessible and efficient with features like:

- **Text-Based Editing:** Edit audio and video by modifying the transcription.
- **Overdub:** Generate voiceovers using an AI clone of your voice.
- **Screen Recording:** Capture presentations or tutorials with ease.

Who Should Use Descript?

- **Podcasters:** Edit episodes quickly and accurately.
- **Video Creators:** Simplify video editing with intuitive tools.
- **Educators:** Create instructional content with ease.

Getting Started with Descript

1. **Download the App:** Visit descript.com to install the software.
2. **Import Files:** Upload audio or video content for editing.
3. **Edit via Text:** Modify the transcription to make precise edits.
4. **Export Your Content:** Save the final product in your desired format.

Pro Tips

· Use the Overdub feature to make quick corrections to voiceovers.
· Leverage screen recording for tutorials or explainer videos.

Real-Life Example
**Scenario:** A marketer edits a webinar recording for a product demo.
**Steps:**

1. Import the webinar video into Descript.
2. Remove filler words and trim irrelevant sections.
3. Add captions and export the polished video.

**Result:** A professional demo video ready for sharing with clients and leads.

Final Thoughts
Descript revolutionizes audio and video editing with text-based tools, making content creation faster and more accessible for all.

# III

# Productivity and Business Tools

*AI-powered productivity tools are transforming the way businesses operate by streamlining tasks, enhancing communication, and boosting creativity. From managing ideas and automating coding to providing real-time meeting transcriptions and multilingual support, these tools enable businesses to save time and improve efficiency. By integrating AI into workflows, they empower professionals to focus on innovation and deliver impactful results with ease.*

# 13

# Notion AI – Managing Tasks and Ideas

What is Notion AI?

Notion AI integrates with Notion's popular productivity platform to assist with writing, brainstorming, and organizing your workflow. It's perfect for managing projects, notes, and team collaboration.

Why Use Notion AI?

Notion AI enhances productivity with:

- **Automated Summaries:** Generate summaries of long documents or notes.
- **Task Assistance:** Suggests ideas or organizes project workflows.
- **Content Generation:** Drafts text for reports, emails, or presentations.

Who Should Use Notion AI?

- **Teams:** Collaborate efficiently with shared workspaces.
- **Freelancers:** Keep track of projects and deadlines.
- **Entrepreneurs:** Organize business ideas and action plans.

Getting Started with Notion AI

1. **Enable AI Features:** Access Notion AI via your Notion workspace.
2. **Draft Content:** Use AI to brainstorm ideas or generate outlines.
3. **Organize Projects:** Create task lists and assign priorities.

Pro Tips

- Integrate Notion AI with other apps for seamless task management.
- Use AI to create templates for recurring projects.

Real-Life Example

**Scenario:** An entrepreneur plans a product launch.

**Steps:**

1. Create a project timeline in Notion.
2. Use AI to outline a marketing strategy.
3. Assign tasks to team members and track progress.

**Result:** A well-organized plan that keeps everyone aligned.

Final Thoughts

Notion AI enhances productivity by automating task management and content generation, making it an essential tool for efficient workflows and organized collaboration.

# 14

# GitHub Copilot – Coding Smarter

What is GitHub Copilot?

GitHub Copilot is an AI-powered code assistant that suggests code snippets and automates repetitive tasks. It integrates seamlessly with popular code editors like Visual Studio Code.

Why Use GitHub Copilot?

Copilot accelerates development workflows with features like:

- **Code Suggestions:** Autocomplete entire functions or lines of code.
- **Error Reduction:** Helps avoid syntax errors and bugs.
- **Learning Support:** Offers code explanations and learning opportunities.

Who Should Use GitHub Copilot?

- **Developers:** Speed up coding tasks and improve efficiency.
- **Students:** Learn coding faster with helpful suggestions.
- **Entrepreneurs:** Build prototypes or small-scale applications quickly.

Getting Started with GitHub Copilot

1. **Install the Extension:** Add GitHub Copilot to your code editor.
2. **Start Coding:** Write a comment or start a function to receive suggestions.
3. **Refine Outputs:** Adjust suggested code to fit your requirements.

Pro Tips

- Use comments to guide Copilot's suggestions.
- Combine Copilot with code reviews to ensure quality.

Real-Life Example
**Scenario:** A developer creates a simple chatbot.
**Steps:**

1. Write a comment describing the chatbot's functionality.
2. Use Copilot's suggestions to complete the code.
3. Test and refine the chatbot.

**Result:** A functional chatbot prototype developed in record time.

Final Thoughts
GitHub Copilot accelerates coding by providing intelligent suggestions, making development faster, more efficient, and accessible to programmers of all skill levels.

# 15

# Tidio AI: Enhancing Customer Support with Chatbots

What is Tidio AI?

Tidio AI is a customer service platform that uses AI-powered chatbots to automate and enhance interactions with customers. It helps businesses provide quick, personalized responses to inquiries, improving customer satisfaction and reducing response times.

Why Use Tidio AI?

- **Automated Responses:** Handle frequent customer inquiries with pre-built chatbot templates.
- **24/7 Availability:** Ensure customer support is available around the clock.
- **Personalized Interactions:** Use AI to deliver tailored responses based on customer behavior.
- **Integration Friendly:** Seamlessly integrate with popular platforms like Shopify, WordPress, and Messenger.

Who Should Use Tidio AI?

- **Small Businesses:** Improve efficiency by automating routine customer queries.
- **E-Commerce Stores:** Provide instant answers about orders, returns, and product availability.
- **Service Providers:** Manage appointment scheduling and common requests with ease.

Getting Started with Tidio AI

1. **Sign Up:** Create an account at tidio.com.
2. **Set Up Your Chatbot:** Use templates or customize a chatbot to handle common inquiries.
3. **Integrate with Platforms:** Connect Tidio to your website, e-commerce store, or social media platforms.
4. **Monitor and Improve:** Use analytics to track chatbot performance and customer satisfaction.

Pro Tips

- Use Tidio AI's live chat feature for complex queries that require human intervention.
- Customize chatbot workflows to guide customers toward purchases or resolutions effectively.
- Leverage its multilingual capabilities to engage with a global audience.

Real-Life Example

**Scenario:** An e-commerce store wants to improve response times during peak shopping seasons.

**Steps:**

1. Set up a Tidio chatbot to handle FAQs like shipping times and return policies.
2. Integrate with the store's Shopify platform to track orders and answer customer inquiries.
3. Use analytics to identify trends and improve the chatbot's responses over time.

**Result:** Customers receive instant support, improving satisfaction and increasing conversions during busy sales periods.

Final Thoughts

Tidio AI empowers businesses to enhance customer service with AI-driven automation, ensuring faster, more efficient interactions. It's a valuable tool for improving customer satisfaction and streamlining support workflows.

# 16

# Otter.ai: Automatic Meeting Transcriptions

What is Otter.ai?

Otter.ai is an AI-powered transcription tool that captures and converts spoken words into written text in real time. It simplifies note-taking and meeting documentation, making it a vital tool for professionals and teams.

Why Use Otter.ai?

- **Real-Time Transcriptions:** Capture conversations during meetings, interviews, or lectures.
- **Speaker Identification:** Distinguish between multiple speakers for clarity.
- **Seamless Integration:** Connect with platforms like Zoom, Google Meet, and Microsoft Teams.
- **Searchable Notes:** Easily find specific information with keyword searches.

Who Should Use Otter.ai?

- **Professionals:** Document meetings and share notes with teams.
- **Students:** Record and review lectures or study sessions.
- **Content Creators:** Transcribe interviews or discussions for blogs and articles.

Getting Started with Otter.ai

1. **Sign Up:** Create an account at otter.ai.
2. **Connect Your Tools:** Sync Otter.ai with meeting platforms like Zoom or upload recorded audio files.
3. **Transcribe:** Use Otter.ai to generate real-time or post-meeting transcripts.
4. **Organize and Share:** Save and share transcripts with collaborators or team members.

Pro Tips

- Use Otter.ai's live transcription feature during meetings to ensure everyone has access to the discussion.
- Highlight and annotate key points in the transcript for easy reference later.
- Utilize its mobile app for on-the-go transcriptions.

Real-Life Example

**Scenario:** A team leader wants to ensure no key points are missed during a brainstorming session.

**Steps:**

1. Use Otter.ai to transcribe the meeting in real time.
2. Share the transcript with team members immediately after the session.

3. Highlight actionable items and assign tasks based on the discussion.

**Result:** The team saves time on manual note-taking, ensuring everyone stays aligned on priorities.

Final Thoughts

Otter.ai is a powerful tool for capturing and organizing conversations, enhancing collaboration and productivity. Its real-time transcription capabilities make it indispensable for professionals and students alike

# 17

# DeepL: High-Quality Translation for Business Needs

What is DeepL?

DeepL is an AI-powered translation tool known for its accuracy and natural-sounding translations. It's designed to help businesses and professionals communicate effectively across languages, making it a top choice for global collaboration.

Why Use DeepL?

- **Accurate Translations:** Provides high-quality translations that maintain the original text's context and tone.
- **Wide Language Support:** Covers multiple languages with nuanced precision.
- **File Translation:** Upload documents like PDFs and Word files for instant translation.
- **Customizable Glossaries:** Define terms to maintain consistency in specialized translations.

Who Should Use DeepL?

- **Businesses:** Communicate seamlessly with international clients and partners.
- **Content Creators:** Localize blogs, websites, and marketing materials.
- **Students and Researchers:** Translate academic texts with clarity and accuracy.

Getting Started with DeepL

1. **Visit the Platform:** Access DeepL at deepl.com and choose your language pair.
2. **Input Text:** Paste text or upload files for translation.
3. **Review and Edit:** Use the editor to refine translations as needed.
4. **Download Translated Files:** Save and share translated documents instantly.

Pro Tips

- Use the Pro version for enhanced features like unlimited file translations and API integration.
- Customize the glossary for specialized terminology or brand-specific phrases.
- Combine with other localization tools for global marketing campaigns.

Real-Life Example

**Scenario:** A business owner wants to localize their e-commerce website for a German audience.

**Steps:**

1. Use DeepL to translate product descriptions and website text into

German.

2. Review and adjust translations using the customizable glossary.

3. Launch the localized website to attract German-speaking customers.

**Result:** The business expands its reach and improves engagement with a global audience.

Final Thoughts

DeepL combines accuracy and ease of use, making it an indispensable tool for businesses and professionals working across languages. Its reliable translations help bridge communication gaps and foster global connections.

# 18

# HyperWrite: Boosting Creativity in Writing

What is HyperWrite?

HyperWrite is an AI-powered writing assistant that helps users generate ideas, craft engaging content, and overcome creative blocks. It's a versatile tool for writers, marketers, and professionals seeking to enhance their writing productivity.

Why Use HyperWrite?

- **Content Suggestions:** Generate ideas, outlines, or complete sentences for various writing tasks.
- **Creative Assistance:** Brainstorm unique angles and refine drafts effortlessly.
- **Time Efficiency:** Accelerate the writing process without sacrificing quality.
- **Customizable Tone:** Adjust the tone and style to fit your specific needs.

Who Should Use HyperWrite?

- **Writers:** Generate content ideas and polish drafts for blogs, articles,

or fiction.
- **Marketers:** Create engaging ad copy, social media posts, and emails.
- **Students and Professionals:** Simplify essays, reports, and presentations.

## Getting Started with HyperWrite

1. **Sign Up:** Create an account at hyperwrite.ai.
2. **Choose a Task:** Specify what you need—idea generation, drafting, or editing.
3. **Review Suggestions:** Select and refine AI-generated content to match your intent.
4. **Incorporate Outputs:** Use the finalized content in your projects.

## Pro Tips

- Use HyperWrite's brainstorming features for complex projects like storytelling or brand campaigns.
- Experiment with different prompts to explore creative possibilities.
- Combine HyperWrite with editing tools for flawless final drafts.

## Real-Life Example

**Scenario:** A marketer needs engaging captions for a new product launch.

**Steps:**

1. Enter prompts describing the product's features and target audience.
2. Review and select AI-generated captions.
3. Refine the tone to align with the brand voice and post them on social media.

**Result:** The marketer creates high-quality captions quickly, boosting engagement with minimal effort.

Final Thoughts

HyperWrite empowers users to unlock their creative potential by providing smart suggestions and streamlining the writing process. It's a must-have tool for anyone seeking to produce high-quality content efficiently.

# IV

# Specialized and Niche Tools

*Specialized AI tools cater to unique needs, offering advanced solutions for specific tasks. They assist with research, automate repetitive workflows, enable personalized interactions, and provide computational insights. From enhancing academic productivity to creating engaging conversations and managing digital memories, these tools streamline complex processes and open up new possibilities for professionals and innovators in niche fields.*

# 19

# Elicit – Research Assistance for Academics and Professionals

*What is Elicit?*

Elicit is an AI research assistant designed to help academics, students, and professionals streamline the process of finding, summarizing, and organizing research papers. It uses AI to analyze and extract relevant information from large datasets or publications.

Why Use Elicit?

Elicit makes research more efficient with features like:

- **Paper Summaries:** Get concise summaries of academic articles.
- **Question Answering:** Find answers to research questions directly from academic sources.
- **Data Organization:** Organize findings into structured formats.

Who Should Use Elicit?

- **Academics and Researchers:** Save time on literature reviews.

- **Students:** Simplify the process of finding credible sources for assignments.
- **Professionals:** Use data-driven insights to inform business or technical decisions.

Getting Started with Elicit

1. **Sign Up:** Visit elicit.org and create an account.
2. **Ask a Question:** Input your research query or topic of interest.
3. **Review Results:** Analyze the AI-curated papers and summaries.
4. **Organize Data:** Use Elicit's tools to format findings for easy reference.

Pro Tips

- Use Elicit for rapid systematic reviews in academic or business research.
- Combine with citation management tools for a seamless workflow.

Real-Life Example

**Scenario:** A graduate student needs to gather studies on renewable energy.

**Steps:**

1. Enter the query, "What are the latest advancements in renewable energy storage?"
2. Review the top papers suggested by Elicit.
3. Summarize findings in a presentation for class.

**Result:** Hours of manual research are reduced to minutes.

Final Thoughts

Elicit streamlines research by providing quick access to summaries, insights, and relevant academic papers, saving time and boosting efficiency.

# 20

# Bardeen – Automating Repetitive Online Tasks

What is Bardeen?

Why Use Bardeen?

Bardeen helps save time and reduces effort with:

- **Browser Automation:** Automate tasks like data entry, form submissions, and scraping.
- **App Integrations:** Connect with tools like Notion, Slack, and Google Sheets.
- **Pre-Built Workflows:** Use ready-made recipes for common tasks.

Who Should Use Bardeen?

- **Professionals:** Automate data transfer between apps.
- **Marketers:** Collect data or manage CRM updates effortlessly.
- **Developers:** Simplify repetitive testing or debugging tasks.

Getting Started with Bardeen

1. **Install the Extension:** Add Bardeen to your browser from bardeen.ai.
2. **Choose a Recipe:** Select a pre-built automation or create your own.
3. **Run the Task:** Activate the automation and let Bardeen handle the rest.

Pro Tips

- Customize workflows for tasks like scraping data from websites or sending automated emails.
- Combine with productivity tools to boost team efficiency.

Real-Life Example

**Scenario:** A marketer wants to scrape competitor prices and update a Google Sheet.

**Steps:**

1. Use Bardeen to scrape prices from a competitor's website.
2. Automate data entry into a Google Sheet.
3. Schedule the task to run weekly.

**Result:** Competitive pricing data is kept up to date automatically.

Final Thoughts

Bardeen automates repetitive online tasks, improving productivity and freeing up time for more critical and creative activities.

# 21

# Character.AI: Personalized Conversations and Entertainment

**What is Character.AI?**

Character.AI is a platform that lets users interact with customizable AI personalities, enabling engaging and unique conversations. It's designed for entertainment, creative exploration, and practical applications like brainstorming or testing ideas.

**Why Use Character.AI?**

- **Custom Personalities:** Create AI characters with specific traits and knowledge areas.
- **Interactive Experiences:** Engage in dynamic conversations for entertainment or learning.
- **Creative Exploration:** Use the platform to brainstorm ideas or role-play scenarios.

**Who Should Use Character.AI?**

- **Writers and Storytellers:** Develop dialogue or character arcs for creative projects.
- **Educators and Learners:** Build teaching assistants or explore conversational learning.
- **Gamers and Hobbyists:** Design interactive characters for games or personal enjoyment.

## Getting Started with Character.AI

1. **Sign Up:** Visit character.ai and create an account.
2. **Design a Character:** Customize traits, behaviors, and expertise for your AI.
3. **Interact:** Chat with your character to test its responses or enjoy conversations.
4. **Refine:** Adjust settings to improve interactions or tailor the character further.

## Pro Tips

- Use Character.AI for brainstorming or testing dialogue for stories or scripts.
- Share your AI characters with friends or collaborators for feedback.

## Real-Life Example

**Scenario:** A game developer designs an AI character to test dialogue for a new RPG.

**Steps:**

1. Customize an AI character with personality traits and a backstory.
2. Interact with the character to simulate in-game conversations.
3. Refine the dialogue based on the AI's responses for better player

engagement.

**Result:** The developer creates more natural and immersive dialogue, enhancing the game's narrative quality.

Final Thoughts

Character.AI brings creativity to life with customizable conversations, making it a valuable tool for storytelling, learning, and entertainment. It's perfect for anyone looking to experiment with interactive and dynamic AI.

# 22

# Wolfram Alpha - Computational Insights and Solutions

## What is Wolfram Alpha?

Wolfram Alpha is a computational knowledge engine that provides answers and solutions to complex queries. From math problems to financial data analysis, it's a go-to tool for professionals and students.

## Why Use Wolfram Alpha?

Wolfram Alpha simplifies problem-solving with:

- **Instant Calculations:** Solve equations or analyze datasets quickly.
- **Expert-Level Answers:** Access detailed insights in science, engineering, and business.
- **Custom Reports:** Generate reports with step-by-step explanations.

## Who Should Use Wolfram Alpha?

- **Students:** Solve homework problems or prepare for exams.
- **Researchers:** Analyze data or validate findings.
- **Professionals:** Use computational tools for decision-making.

Getting Started with Wolfram Alpha

1. **Visit the Website:** Go to wolframalpha.com.
2. **Enter a Query:** Input your question or problem.
3. **Review Results:** Analyze the detailed response and explore related insights.

Pro Tips

· Use the pro version for advanced features like step-by-step solutions.
· Combine with spreadsheets for enhanced data analysis.

Real-Life Example
**Scenario:** A financial analyst needs to model investment growth.
**Steps:**

1. Enter the query, "Calculate compound interest for $10,000 at 5% over 10 years."
2. Review the detailed breakdown.
3. Export results to include in a report.

**Result:** The analyst completes the task accurately and quickly.

Final Thoughts
Character.AI enables engaging and customized AI-driven conversations, offering both entertainment and practical applications for creativity and learning.

# 23

# Rewind AI – A Digital Memory Assistant

What is Rewind AI?

Rewind AI is a digital memory tool that records and organizes your digital activities, making it easy to recall past interactions, documents, or meetings.

Why Use Rewind AI?

Rewind AI enhances productivity with:

- **Searchable Memory:** Quickly find past conversations or files.
- **Privacy Controls:** Store data securely and control what is recorded.
- **Meeting Insights:** Automatically capture and summarize key points.

Who Should Use Rewind AI?

- **Professionals:** Manage busy schedules and recall critical details.
- **Students:** Keep track of lecture notes and research activities.
- **Entrepreneurs:** Access past communications for strategic decision-making.

Getting Started with Rewind AI

1. **Install the App:** Download Rewind AI to your device.
2. **Customize Settings:** Select what activities to record.
3. **Search and Recall:** Use the search bar to find specific information.

Pro Tips

- Use Rewind AI to revisit meeting discussions and prepare follow-ups.
- Set privacy filters to exclude sensitive data from recording.

Real-Life Example

**Scenario:** A manager needs to recall details from a client call.

**Steps:**

1. Search for the client's name in Rewind AI.
2. Review the recorded conversation.
3. Extract key points for a follow-up email.

**Result:** The manager saves time and ensures accurate communication.

Final Thoughts

Rewind AI is a powerful digital memory tool that helps users effortlessly capture, organize, and recall past interactions and information. Its ability to streamline productivity and improve focus makes it an invaluable resource for professionals and anyone looking to manage their digital activities efficiently.

# V

# AI for Selling and Marketing

*AI tools are transforming selling and marketing by automating processes, optimizing ad campaigns, and enhancing creativity. They simplify e-commerce management, streamline dropshipping, and leverage trends for impactful marketing. From crafting engaging copy to generating high-performing ads, these tools empower businesses to reach their audiences effectively, save time, and drive sales with data-driven precision.*

# 24

# Shopify – Streamlining Your E-Commerce Business

What is Shopify?

Shopify is an all-in-one e-commerce platform that enables entrepreneurs to create, manage, and scale their online stores. It simplifies everything from inventory management to payment processing, making it a top choice for small and medium-sized businesses.

Why Use Shopify?

Shopify provides powerful tools to streamline your e-commerce operations, including:

- **User-Friendly Store Builder:** Create a professional online store with customizable templates.
- **Payment Integration:** Accept multiple payment methods securely.
- **Marketing Features:** Run campaigns and track sales performance in one place.

Who Should Use Shopify?

- **Entrepreneurs:** Launch a new online business with minimal effort.

- **Small Business Owners:** Scale operations with advanced tools.
- **Creators:** Monetize products like digital art, merchandise, or subscriptions.

## Getting Started with Shopify

1. **Sign Up:** Visit shopify.com to create an account.
2. **Set Up Your Store:** Choose a template and customize your store-front.
3. **Add Products:** Upload product descriptions, images, and pricing.
4. **Launch:** Set up payment methods and publish your store.

## Pro Tips

- Use Shopify's analytics to track customer behavior and optimize sales.
- Integrate apps for email marketing, shipping, and inventory management.

## Real-Life Example

**Scenario:** A craft maker wants to sell handmade goods online.
**Steps:**

1. Create a Shopify store and upload product images.
2. Use Shopify's SEO tools to optimize product pages.
3. Promote the store through social media integrations.

**Result:** The craft maker increases reach and sales while managing orders efficiently.

## Final Thoughts

Shopify is a comprehensive solution for creating and managing an online store, empowering entrepreneurs to scale their businesses efficiently with powerful tools and seamless integrations.

# 25

# AutoDS: Automating Your Dropshipping Business

What is AutoDS?

AutoDS is a comprehensive dropshipping platform that streamlines product sourcing, order fulfillment, and inventory management for e-commerce stores. Designed for efficiency, AutoDS automates repetitive tasks, helping entrepreneurs focus on scaling their businesses.

Why Use AutoDS?

- **Product Sourcing:** Access products from a wide network of suppliers, including AliExpress, Amazon, Walmart, and eBay.
- **Inventory and Price Automation:** Monitor and update inventory and pricing in real-time to prevent overselling or pricing errors.
- **Order Fulfillment:** Automate order processing and shipment tracking for a seamless customer experience.
- **AI Product Research:** Leverage AI tools to identify high-demand, profitable products.
- **Multi-Platform Support:** Works with Shopify, WooCommerce, Wix,

and other platforms.

## Who Should Use AutoDS?

- **E-Commerce Entrepreneurs:** Start or scale a dropshipping business with minimal manual effort.
- **Shopify Store Owners:** Enhance store management with advanced automation features.
- **Small Business Owners:** Streamline inventory and order processes for better efficiency.

## Getting Started with AutoDS

1. **Sign Up:** Create an account at autods.com.
2. **Integrate Your Store:** Connect AutoDS to your Shopify or other e-commerce platform.
3. **Import Products:** Choose products from supported suppliers and import them directly to your store.
4. **Automate Operations:** Set up price and stock monitoring, order fulfillment, and customer notifications.
5. **Analyze and Optimize:** Use AutoDS analytics to track performance and refine your strategy.

## Pro Tips

- Use AutoDS's bulk importing feature to quickly populate your store with high-demand products.
- Leverage their product research tool to identify trending items in your niche.
- Enable automatic returns management to improve customer satisfaction.

Real-Life Example

**Scenario:** A Shopify store owner wants to scale operations while managing multiple suppliers.

**Steps:**

1. Connect their Shopify store to AutoDS.
2. Import products from multiple suppliers, including Amazon and Walmart.
3. Automate price adjustments and inventory tracking to avoid over-selling.

**Result:** The store operates more efficiently, allowing the owner to focus on marketing and growth.

Final Thoughts

AutoDS is a powerful dropshipping tool that simplifies and automates the most time-consuming aspects of e-commerce. Its wide supplier network, advanced automation, and multi-platform support make it a valuable resource for entrepreneurs looking to streamline operations and scale their businesses effectively.

# 26

# TikTok Creative Center – Leveraging Trends for Marketing Success

What is TikTok Creative Center?

TikTok Creative Center provides insights and tools to help businesses create trend-savvy content and run effective marketing campaigns on TikTok. It's designed to maximize reach and engagement by leveraging real-time trends and analytics.

Why Use TikTok Creative Center?

TikTok Creative Center helps businesses tap into the platform's immense audience with:

- **Trend Analysis:** Stay updated on trending hashtags, sounds, and challenges.
- **Ad Creation Tools:** Access templates and tips for crafting effective TikTok ads.
- **Performance Insights:** Analyze campaign metrics to refine strategies.

Who Should Use TikTok Creative Center?

- **Marketers:** Create viral campaigns that resonate with audiences.
- **Small Business Owners:** Promote products and services to a younger demographic.
- **Content Creators:** Leverage TikTok's tools to grow and monetize their following.

Getting Started with TikTok Creative Center

1. **Access the Platform:** Visit TikTok Creative Center.
2. **Explore Trends:** Research trending topics, sounds, and hashtags.
3. **Create Content:** Use templates and AI tools to craft engaging videos.
4. **Run Ads:** Launch campaigns targeting specific audiences.

Pro Tips

- Monitor trending hashtags regularly to stay relevant.
- Use TikTok's AI tools to create dynamic and engaging ad content.

Real-Life Example
**Scenario:** A clothing brand wants to launch a TikTok campaign for a new collection.
**Steps:**

1. Research trending sounds and challenges using TikTok Creative Center.
2. Create videos featuring the new collection with engaging captions.
3. Launch a campaign targeting fashion enthusiasts.

**Result:** Increased brand visibility and a boost in sales.

Final Thoughts

TikTok Creative Center helps businesses stay relevant by leveraging trending content and analytics, making it a valuable resource for crafting impactful and engaging marketing campaigns.

# 27

# AdCreative.ai (Revisited) - Optimizing Ads for Sales

Why Revisit AdCreative.ai?

In addition to its role in designing visually appealing ads, AdCreative.ai offers advanced tools to optimize ads for sales. By analyzing performance data and generating tailored suggestions, it ensures your campaigns deliver maximum ROI.

Key Features for Optimization

- **Performance Metrics:** Evaluate ad success through detailed analytics.
- **A/B Testing:** Quickly compare variations to identify what works best.
- **Personalized Recommendations:** Tailored improvements based on campaign goals.

Getting the Most from AdCreative.ai

1. **Analyze Past Campaigns:** Use performance data to identify strengths and weaknesses.

2. **Optimize Visuals and Copy:** Refine ads based on AI-generated insights.
3. **Test and Adjust:** Run new campaigns with A/B testing for continued improvement.

Real-Life Example

**Scenario:** A small business wants to improve Facebook ad conversions.
**Steps:**

1. Review analytics for previous campaigns.
2. Adjust visuals and headlines based on AdCreative.ai's suggestions.
3. Test two ad variations and select the higher-performing one.

**Result:** Improved ad performance and a noticeable increase in conversions.

Final Thoughts

AdCreative.ai enhances ad performance by generating data-driven creatives and copy, ensuring businesses achieve higher engagement and conversions effortlessly.

# 28

# Jasper.ai – Crafting Engaging Marketing Copy

What is Jasper.ai?

Jasper.ai is a content creation tool powered by AI, designed to help businesses craft compelling marketing copy. From social media posts to blog articles, Jasper saves time and ensures high-quality output.

Why Use Jasper.ai?

Jasper.ai enhances your marketing strategy with:

- **AI-Generated Copy:** Create ads, emails, and more with minimal input.
- **Tone Customization:** Adjust writing style to suit your brand voice.
- **SEO Optimization:** Generate content designed to rank well on search engines.

Who Should Use Jasper.ai?

- **Marketers:** Produce content for campaigns quickly and efficiently.
- **Entrepreneurs:** Draft professional communications with ease.
- **Bloggers:** Generate SEO-friendly posts in less time.

Getting Started with Jasper.ai

1. **Sign Up:** Visit jasper.ai and create an account.
2. **Input Your Needs:** Describe the content type and topic.
3. **Review Outputs:** Refine AI-generated content to align with your goals.
4. **Publish:** Use the content in your campaigns or platforms.

Pro Tips

- Use Jasper.ai for idea generation and content outlines.
- Combine with SEO tools for maximum visibility.

Real-Life Example

**Scenario:** A marketer needs a compelling email for a product launch.

**Steps:**

1. Input the product details and desired tone into Jasper.ai.
2. Review and edit the generated email copy.
3. Send the email to a segmented list of potential customers.

**Result:** A professionally written email that drives engagement and conversions.

Final Thoughts

Jasper.ai empowers marketers and creators to produce compelling, SEO-friendly content quickly, making it a must-have tool for scaling content marketing strategies.

# 29

# Forethought: AI for Customer Support

What is Forethought?

Forethought is an AI-powered platform designed to enhance customer support by automating ticket resolution and improving response times. By leveraging advanced machine learning, Forethought helps businesses provide faster, smarter, and more efficient customer service. Its tools integrate seamlessly with popular help desk platforms, enabling companies to deliver exceptional support experiences.

Why Use Forethought?

- **Automated Ticket Resolution:** Quickly resolve common issues with AI-powered workflows.
- **Intelligent Suggestions:** Provide agents with context-relevant responses to improve accuracy.
- **Seamless Integration:** Works with platforms like Zendesk, Salesforce, and HubSpot.
- **Data-Driven Insights:** Analyze support trends to identify areas for improvement.

## Who Should Use Forethought?

- **Support Teams:** Streamline workflows and handle customer inquiries more efficiently.
- **Businesses:** Scale customer service without increasing headcount.
- **Startups:** Provide professional support even with limited resources.

## Getting Started with Forethought

1. **Sign Up:** Create an account at forethought.ai.
2. **Integrate with Help Desk Tools:** Connect Forethought to your existing support platform.
3. **Set Up Workflows:** Configure AI workflows to resolve common customer queries automatically.
4. **Train AI Models:** Use historical data to improve Forethought's accuracy in understanding and resolving tickets.
5. **Monitor Performance:** Track metrics to measure efficiency and customer satisfaction.

## Pro Tips

- Use Forethought's AI-powered search to deliver faster resolutions by pulling relevant information instantly.
- Train the system regularly with new data to ensure continuous improvement.
- Analyze customer feedback to refine support workflows and enhance user satisfaction.

## Real-Life Example

**Scenario:** A growing e-commerce company faces a high volume of support tickets during holiday sales.

**Steps:**

1. Implement Forethought to automate responses for FAQs, such as shipping times and return policies.
2. Train AI models using past ticket data to improve accuracy.
3. Provide agents with suggested responses for complex queries.

**Result:** The company reduces ticket resolution times, improves customer satisfaction, and manages the holiday rush efficiently without increasing staff.

Final Thoughts

Forethought empowers businesses to deliver smarter, faster, and more effective customer support. By automating repetitive tasks and providing actionable insights, it enables support teams to focus on resolving complex issues and enhancing the overall customer experience. It's a powerful tool for scaling support operations and maintaining high service standards.

# VI

# AI for Voice and Audio

*AI tools for voice and audio enhance communication and content creation with innovative solutions. From generating lifelike voiceovers and professional audio to removing background noise and editing audio with ease, these tools streamline production. They also offer transcription and custom voice options, making them essential for businesses, creators, and professionals seeking to deliver clear, engaging, and accessible audio content.*

# 30

# Speechify : Professional Audio Content Creation

What is Speechify?

Speechify is an AI-powered tool that converts written text into high-quality audio. Designed to enhance accessibility and productivity, it allows users to listen to books, documents, emails, and web pages instead of reading them. It's a perfect solution for those who prefer auditory learning or need assistance due to visual impairments or dyslexia.

Why Use Speechify?

- **Natural-Sounding Voices:** Choose from a variety of realistic AI voices and languages.
- **Custom Playback Settings:** Adjust the reading speed and voice tone to fit your preference.
- **Versatile Input Sources:** Convert text from PDFs, Word documents, web pages, and more.
- **Accessibility Features:** Makes content accessible to those with

reading challenges or visual impairments.

Who Should Use Speechify?

- **Students:** Convert textbooks and notes into audio for on-the-go studying.
- **Professionals:** Stay productive by listening to emails and reports during commutes.
- **Writers and Readers:** Enjoy audiobooks by converting eBooks and articles into speech.
- **Individuals with Accessibility Needs:** Use it as a reading aid for dyslexia or visual impairments.

Getting Started with Speechify

1. **Download the App:** Install Speechify from speechify.com or your app store.
2. **Upload Text:** Import documents, paste text, or use the browser extension for web content.
3. **Choose a Voice:** Select a voice and language that suits your needs.
4. **Play and Listen:** Press play to enjoy content in audio format.

Pro Tips

- Use Speechify to speed up your learning by listening to content at a faster playback rate.
- Integrate it with cloud storage platforms like Google Drive or Dropbox for easy access to files.
- Leverage the browser extension to listen to online articles without interruptions.

Real-Life Example

**Scenario:** A student with a packed schedule struggles to read through all assigned material.

**Steps:**

1. Upload their textbooks and notes into Speechify.
2. Choose a natural-sounding voice and adjust the playback speed for faster listening.
3. Listen to the material while commuting or exercising.

**Result:** The student efficiently absorbs more content without sacrificing their time or energy.

Final Thoughts

Speechify is a versatile and powerful tool that transforms text into audio, making content more accessible and productive for users. Whether you're a student, professional, or someone with unique accessibility needs, Speechify empowers you to engage with written material in a way that suits your lifestyle.

# 31

# Krisp: Removing Background Noise for Clear Communication

What is Krisp?

Krisp is an AI-powered noise cancellation app designed to remove background noise during calls and recordings in real-time. It enhances audio clarity, ensuring professional communication and content creation.

Why Use Krisp?

- **Noise Cancellation:** Eliminates distracting sounds like keyboard clicks, traffic, or barking dogs.
- **Improved Audio Quality:** Ensures clear and uninterrupted conversations or recordings.
- **Multi-Platform Compatibility:** Works seamlessly with popular apps like Zoom, Microsoft Teams, and Slack.
- **User-Friendly Interface:** One-click activation for instant improvement in audio quality.

Who Should Use Krisp?

- **Remote Workers:** Maintain professionalism during virtual meetings in noisy environments.
- **Content Creators:** Record high-quality podcasts, videos, or tutorials.
- **Educators and Trainers:** Deliver clear, distraction-free online classes.

Getting Started with Krisp

1. **Install the App:** Download Krisp from krisp.ai and set it up.
2. **Activate Noise Cancellation:** Enable the feature during calls or recordings.
3. **Integrate with Tools:** Use Krisp with your preferred communication or recording apps.
4. **Enjoy Clear Communication:** Experience distraction-free audio in any environment.

Pro Tips

- Pair Krisp with a good-quality microphone for even better results.
- Utilize echo cancellation to enhance clarity in less acoustically optimized spaces.
- Use Krisp's analytics to monitor audio performance and settings.

Real-Life Example

**Scenario:** A remote team member joins a virtual meeting from a busy café.

**Steps:**

1. Activate Krisp to cancel background noise during the call.
2. Speak clearly without worrying about surrounding distractions.

3. Collaborate effectively without audio issues.

**Result:** The team member communicates professionally, regardless of the noisy environment.

Final Thoughts

Krisp ensures crystal-clear communication by removing background noise in real-time. It's an essential tool for professionals, educators, and content creators who value high-quality audio in any setting.

# 32

# Murf.ai: Generating Lifelike Voiceovers

What is Murf.ai?

Murf.ai is an AI-powered platform for creating professional-grade voiceovers. It provides lifelike voice options in multiple languages, making it ideal for videos, presentations, ads, and eLearning content.

Why Use Murf.ai?

- **Wide Voice Selection:** Choose from various voices, accents, and tones to suit your project.
- **Customizable Features:** Adjust pitch, speed, and emphasis for a natural flow.
- **Multi-Language Support:** Produce voiceovers in different languages for a global audience.
- **Time and Cost Efficiency:** Save time and resources compared to hiring voice actors.

Who Should Use Murf.ai?

- **Content Creators:** Add professional narration to YouTube videos, tutorials, and podcasts.
- **Marketers:** Create engaging voiceovers for ads and promotional videos.
- **Educators:** Enhance eLearning modules with clear and engaging narration.

Getting Started with Murf.ai

1. **Sign Up:** Create an account at murf.ai.
2. **Upload or Write a Script:** Provide the text for your voiceover.
3. **Select a Voice:** Choose from the available options to match your project's tone.
4. **Customize and Export:** Adjust settings and download your finished voiceover.

Pro Tips

- Use Murf.ai's voice cloning feature to create a consistent brand voice.
- Test different voice options to find the one that best suits your audience.
- Leverage the multi-language capabilities for creating multilingual content.

Real-Life Example

**Scenario:** A startup creates a product demo video to explain its new software.

**Steps:**

1. Write a concise script for the demo.
2. Use Murf.ai to generate a professional voiceover in the desired tone.

3. Sync the voiceover with visuals to produce a polished demo video.

**Result:** The startup delivers a professional video that effectively communicates its value to potential customers.

Final Thoughts

Murf.ai simplifies the process of creating high-quality, lifelike voiceovers, making it an invaluable tool for anyone looking to produce professional audio content quickly and affordably.

# 33

# Descript (Revisited): Audio and Voice Editing

What is Descript?

Descript is a versatile audio and video editing platform that enables users to edit content using text-based tools. Its Overdub feature allows for lifelike voice editing and creation, making it ideal for podcasts, videos, and voiceovers.

Why Use Descript?

- **Text-Based Editing:** Modify audio by editing the transcript.
- **Overdub Feature:** Create or correct voiceovers seamlessly with AI.
- **Multi-Tool Integration:** Record, edit, and produce in a single platform.
- **Collaboration Friendly:** Work with team members in real-time.

Who Should Use Descript?

- **Podcasters:** Simplify episode editing and remove filler words.
- **Video Creators:** Combine text and video editing for streamlined

workflows.

- **Businesses:** Produce training or promotional content efficiently.

Getting Started with Descript

1. **Sign Up:** Download Descript at descript.com.
2. **Import Content:** Upload audio or video files for transcription and editing.
3. **Edit Text:** Make changes directly in the transcript to reflect in the audio or video.
4. **Export:** Save the final project in your preferred format.

Pro Tips

- Use Overdub to make quick corrections or create synthetic voiceovers.
- Add captions to increase video accessibility and engagement.
- Use templates for consistent branding in videos.

Real-Life Example

**Scenario:** A podcaster needs to edit an interview for clarity and flow.

**Steps:**

1. Upload the recording to Descript and transcribe it.
2. Remove filler words and edit for clarity using the text editor.
3. Export the polished podcast episode.

**Result:** A professional podcast ready for publishing with minimal effort.

Final Thoughts

Descript revolutionizes content editing by making it text-driven and user-friendly, saving time and enabling high-quality production for creators and businesses alike.

# 34

# Lovo.ai: Custom Voices for Branding

What is Lovo.ai?

Lovo.ai is an AI-powered voice generator that allows users to create custom voiceovers and clone voices for branding purposes. It's an excellent tool for creating unique and consistent audio content across multiple projects.

Why Use Lovo.ai?

- **Voice Cloning:** Create a custom voice for your brand.
- **Multi-Language Support:** Produce voiceovers in various languages.
- **Versatility:** Use for ads, eLearning, audiobooks, and video games.
- **Fast Turnaround:** Generate professional audio quickly and efficiently.

Who Should Use Lovo.ai?

- **Marketers:** Develop branded voices for campaigns.
- **Content Creators:** Create distinct character voices for storytelling.

- **Businesses:** Personalize customer interactions with voice technology.

Getting Started with Lovo.ai

1. **Sign Up:** Create an account at lovo.ai.
2. **Input Your Script:** Provide the text for your voiceover.
3. **Select or Clone a Voice:** Choose an existing voice or create a custom one.
4. **Generate and Download:** Produce the voiceover and export it for use.

Pro Tips

- Use Lovo.ai for multilingual content to expand global reach.
- Leverage voice cloning to maintain consistency in branding across projects.
- Experiment with tones and styles to match your content's needs.

Real-Life Example

**Scenario:** A brand wants to create a distinctive voice for its ad campaign.

**Steps:**

1. Use Lovo.ai to clone a voice that matches the brand's identity.
2. Generate voiceovers for multiple ad scripts in various languages.
3. Incorporate the voiceovers into multimedia marketing materials.

**Result:** A cohesive and professional campaign that enhances brand recognition.

Final Thoughts

Lovo.ai empowers creators and businesses to produce professional-quality voiceovers with ease, offering flexibility and customization for consistent branding and storytelling.

# 35

# Otter.ai (Revisited): Transcriptions for Business and Accessibility

What is Otter.ai?

Otter.ai is an AI-driven transcription service that captures and converts spoken language into text. It simplifies note-taking and improves accessibility for meetings, lectures, and interviews.

Why Use Otter.ai?

- **Real-Time Transcriptions:** Capture conversations instantly.
- **Speaker Identification:** Distinguish between multiple speakers for clarity.
- **Integration Friendly:** Works with platforms like Zoom, Google Meet, and Microsoft Teams.
- **Searchable Notes:** Easily find key points using keyword searches.

Who Should Use Otter.ai?

- **Professionals:** Document meetings and share actionable notes with teams.
- **Students:** Transcribe lectures and study sessions for better reten-

tion.

- **Content Creators:** Turn interviews into transcripts for articles and blogs.

Getting Started with Otter.ai

1. **Create an Account:** Sign up at otter.ai.
2. **Sync Your Tools:** Connect with platforms like Zoom or upload recordings.
3. **Transcribe:** Generate real-time or post-event transcripts.
4. **Organize and Share:** Save and share transcriptions with your team or collaborators.

Pro Tips

- Use Otter.ai's live notes during meetings to enhance collaboration.
- Highlight important sections and add comments to transcripts for clarity.
- Export transcripts in various formats for easy documentation.

Real-Life Example

**Scenario:** A manager wants to document a brainstorming session for follow-up tasks.

**Steps:**

1. Use Otter.ai to transcribe the session in real-time.
2. Highlight actionable items in the transcript.
3. Share the notes with the team to ensure alignment.

**Result:** Improved team productivity and clarity on next steps.

Final Thoughts

Otter.ai simplifies transcription and note-taking, enhancing accessibility and productivity for professionals, students, and teams. Its integration capabilities make it a versatile tool for various use cases.

# VII

# Bonus Section: Apps to Elevate Your Creativity and Content

*These innovative apps take creativity and content creation to the next level. From monetizing your photos and videos with streamlined tools to simplifying book publishing, they offer unique solutions for creators. Whether you're creating lifelike avatars, writing professionally, or integrating climate action into your business, these tools provide fresh opportunities to enhance your projects, engage your audience, and make a meaningful impact.*

# 36

# Wirestock: Simplifying Content Monetization

What is Wirestock?

Wirestock is a content monetization platform that simplifies the process of selling photos, videos, illustrations, and AI-generated art. By acting as a central hub, Wirestock allows creators to upload their work once and distribute it across multiple stock marketplaces like Shutterstock, Adobe Stock, and Alamy, all while automating the submission process.

Why Use Wirestock?

- **One-Click Distribution:** Upload your content once and distribute it to multiple stock libraries simultaneously.

- **Metadata Automation:** AI-powered tools generate keywords, titles, and descriptions, saving time and improving discoverability.

- **Contributor Analytics:** Track the performance of your content and earnings in one place.

- **No Exclusive Contracts:** Retain the freedom to sell your work elsewhere.

Who Should Use Wirestock?

- **Photographers and Videographers:** Monetize creative portfolios efficiently without managing multiple accounts.
- **Artists and Designers:** Sell digital art or illustrations to a global audience.
- **Beginners:** Simplify the complexities of submitting content to various marketplaces.

Getting Started with Wirestock

1. **Sign Up:** Create an account at wirestock.io.
2. **Upload Content:** Add your photos, videos, or digital art to the platform.
3. **Automate Metadata:** Use Wirestock's AI tools to auto-generate metadata for your content.
4. **Submit and Track:** Distribute your work to multiple stock platforms and monitor your sales and performance.

Pro Tips

- Focus on uploading high-quality, unique content to stand out in competitive stock marketplaces.
- Regularly update your portfolio with trending themes or seasonal content.
- Utilize Wirestock's analytics to identify your most successful content and refine your strategy.

Real-Life Example

**Scenario:** A travel photographer wants to maximize earnings from their photo collection.

**Steps:**

1. Upload the photos to Wirestock and use the AI tools for metadata generation.
2. Distribute the content to stock marketplaces like Adobe Stock, Shutterstock, and Alamy.
3. Track downloads and earnings through Wirestock's dashboard.

**Result:** The photographer expands their reach and increases passive income without managing multiple accounts.

Final Thoughts

Wirestock is an excellent solution for creators looking to simplify and maximize content monetization. Its one-click distribution and AI-driven automation make it a valuable tool for photographers, videographers, and digital artists seeking to reach a global audience with minimal effort.

# 37

# Reedsy: Your Partner in Book Writing and Publishing

What is Reedsy?

Reedsy is an all-in-one platform designed for authors and aspiring writers to create, edit, and publish their books. By connecting users with a curated marketplace of publishing professionals, Reedsy simplifies the process of bringing your book from concept to completion.

Why Use Reedsy?

- **Professional Marketplace:** Hire experienced editors, designers, and marketers to enhance your book.
- **Free Book Editor:** Write, format, and organize your manuscript with Reedsy's user-friendly editor.
- **Publishing Guidance:** Access resources to navigate self-publishing or traditional publishing routes.
- **Collaboration Tools:** Work seamlessly with your team in real-time.

Who Should Use Reedsy?

- **Aspiring Authors:** Develop polished manuscripts with professional assistance.
- **Self-Publishers:** Streamline the process of formatting and preparing books for platforms like Amazon Kindle or IngramSpark.
- **Entrepreneurs:** Create and publish business guides, eBooks, or personal brand-building content.

Getting Started with Reedsy

1. **Sign Up:** Create an account at reedsy.com.
2. **Explore the Marketplace:** Browse vetted professionals for editing, cover design, and marketing.
3. **Use the Book Editor:** Start writing or upload your manuscript to format it for publication.
4. **Publish Your Book:** Choose a publishing path and distribute your book to platforms or printers.

Pro Tips

- Use Reedsy's free formatting tools to save on professional layout costs.
- Leverage the platform's resources, like webinars and blogs, for marketing strategies.
- Work with multiple professionals (editors, proofreaders, designers) to refine your book to industry standards.

Real-Life Example

**Scenario:** An entrepreneur wants to publish a business book to establish authority in their field.

**Steps:**

1. Write the manuscript using Reedsy's book editor.
2. Hire a professional editor and cover designer from the Reedsy marketplace.
3. Publish the book through self-publishing platforms with Reedsy's formatting tools.

**Result:** The entrepreneur releases a high-quality, professional book that strengthens their credibility and boosts their brand.

Final Thoughts

Reedsy is a comprehensive platform that empowers authors to create, polish, and publish their work with confidence. Its professional marketplace and easy-to-use tools make it an indispensable resource for writers at any stage of their journey. Whether you're crafting your first novel or publishing a business guide, Reedsy provides the support you need to succeed.

# 38

# Reface: AI-Powered Personal Avatars and Fun Visuals

What is Reface?

Reface is a cutting-edge app that uses AI to create personalized avatars and dynamic visual content. From face-swapping in memes to creating customized video messages, Reface offers engaging tools for entertainment, personal branding, and creative expression.

Why Use Reface?

- **AI Face-Swapping:** Replace faces in trending memes, videos, or GIFs with ease.
- **Custom Avatars:** Create realistic or stylized avatars for personal or professional use.
- **Fun and Engaging:** Share unique and entertaining visuals with friends or audiences.
- **Marketing Applications:** Use creative visuals to make your campaigns stand out.

Who Should Use Reface?

- **Social Media Users:** Create and share trending memes or unique visual content.
- **Marketers:** Add a fun twist to promotional campaigns to boost engagement.
- **Content Creators:** Incorporate personalized visuals into videos or online platforms.

Getting Started with Reface

1. **Download the App:** Install Reface from your app store or visit reface.ai.
2. **Upload Your Photo:** Add your image to start creating custom avatars or face-swapped content.
3. **Explore Templates:** Browse a wide range of videos, GIFs, and memes for customization.
4. **Save and Share:** Export your creations and share them across social media or other platforms.

Pro Tips

- Use Reface for interactive social media content to engage followers.
- Experiment with creative avatars to represent your brand or persona.
- Create personalized video messages to connect with audiences on a deeper level.

Real-Life Example

**Scenario:** A marketer wants to create a viral campaign for a new product launch.

**Steps:**

1. Use Reface to generate face-swapped memes featuring popular movie characters.
2. Share the visuals across social media with creative captions.
3. Encourage followers to create and share their own versions using the app.

**Result:** The campaign gains traction, attracting attention and increasing engagement.

Final Thoughts

Reface combines cutting-edge AI with fun and creativity, making it a versatile tool for entertainment, personal branding, and marketing. Whether you're crafting memes or creating avatars, Reface empowers users to explore unique ways of expressing themselves and connecting with audiences.

# 39

# iPlan.ai: AI-Powered Travel Planning Made Simple

What is iPlan.ai?

iPlan.ai is an innovative app that leverages AI to simplify travel planning. From generating detailed itineraries to managing budgets, iPlan.ai tailors every aspect of your trip based on your preferences. It offers collaborative features, making group travel more organized and stress-free.

Why Use iPlan.ai?

- **Personalized Itineraries**: Generate travel plans tailored to your preferences, destination, and available time.
- **Collaborative Planning**: Plan trips with friends or family, ensuring everyone's needs are accounted for.
- **Budget Management**: Set a budget, and iPlan.ai will suggest accommodations, activities, and transportation within your limits.
- **AI Insights**: Discover hidden gems and off-the-beaten-path experiences with AI-curated recommendations.
- **Real-Time Updates**: Get live updates on flight schedules, weather

conditions, and local transport.

Who Should Use iPlan.ai?

- **Solo Travelers**: Effortlessly plan a personalized adventure without missing out on must-see spots.
- **Group Travelers**: Coordinate schedules, preferences, and expenses for seamless group travel.
- **Busy Professionals**: Save time with AI-generated itineraries and efficient trip organization.
- **Travel Enthusiasts**: Explore unique destinations and create unforgettable experiences with curated recommendations.

Getting Started with iPlan.ai

1. **Sign Up**: Visit iPlan.ai and create an account.
2. **Enter Travel Details**: Input your destination, travel dates, budget, and preferences.
3. **Review Itinerary**: Explore the AI-generated plan, including suggested activities, accommodations, and routes.
4. **Collaborate and Finalize**: Share the plan with others, make adjustments, and confirm bookings.
5. **Download Your Plan**: Save your itinerary for offline access or sync it with your devices.

Pro Tips

- **Maximize Customization**: Input specific interests, like adventure sports or cultural experiences, to get tailored suggestions.
- **Plan Ahead**: Use iPlan.ai to book activities and accommodations early, securing the best rates.

- **Leverage AI Recommendations**: Trust the app to guide you to hidden gems that might not be on mainstream travel lists.

Real-Life Example

**Scenario**: A group of friends wants to plan a two-week European getaway on a budget.

**Steps**:

1. Enter the trip details, including destinations like Paris, Rome, and Barcelona.
2. Set a budget of $1,500 per person.
3. Review the AI-generated itinerary, which includes budget-friendly accommodations, train routes, and affordable dining options.
4. Share the itinerary with friends and finalize bookings.
5. **Result**: The group enjoys a hassle-free, well-organized vacation, with everyone's preferences accounted for.

Final Thoughts

iPlan.ai makes travel planning accessible and efficient, combining advanced AI with user-friendly features. Whether you're a solo adventurer or planning a group getaway, this app empowers you to craft personalized and unforgettable trips with minimal effort. Explore the world with iPlan.ai as your trusted travel companion.

# Conclusion

In today's fast-paced world, leveraging AI tools is no longer a luxury but a necessity for entrepreneurs, creators, and professionals aiming to stay ahead. This toolkit has introduced you to a range of powerful applications designed to enhance productivity, creativity, and efficiency. Whether you're crafting compelling content, streamlining your business operations, or exploring groundbreaking technologies, these tools provide the resources to achieve your goals with less effort and more impact.

The true power of AI lies not only in its capabilities but in how we use it to amplify our strengths and solve problems. By integrating these tools into your workflow, you can focus more on strategic thinking and innovation while automating repetitive tasks. These applications aren't just tools—they're partners in building, scaling, and succeeding in your ventures.

Remember, adopting new technologies is a journey. Start small, experiment, and adapt the tools that align with your needs. As you embrace AI, you'll unlock new opportunities to grow and thrive in ways that were once unimaginable.

The future belongs to those who innovate. With this AI toolkit in your hands, you're equipped to navigate the evolving digital landscape with confidence and creativity. Now, it's time to put these tools into action and create your own success story. The possibilities are limitless—start exploring!

www.ingramcontent.com/pod-product-compliance
Lightning Source LLC
Chambersburg PA
CBHW061735020426
42331CB00006B/1244